# I Failed 1

# I Failed to Swoon

Nadia de Vries

Dostoyevsky Wannabe Originals
*An Imprint of Dostoyevsky Wannabe*

First Published in 2021
by Dostoyevsky Wannabe Originals
All rights reserved
© Nadia de Vries

Dostoyevsky Wannabe Originals is an imprint of
Dostoyevsky Wannabe publishing.

www.dostoyevskywannabe.com

This book is a work of fiction. The names, characters and incidents
portrayed in it are the work of the authors' imagination. Any resemblance
to actual persons, living or dead, events or localities is entirely coincidental.

Cover design by Dostoyevsky Wannabe Design
Interior Design by Tommy Pearson, pomegranateditorial

ISBN-9798516193279

# Contents

*If you can't handle my sickness,
don't trigger my gag reflex.*

## Sicker Than Dogs

I'm so cosmopolitan
I've been to hell and back.
I want to stay at home
Drink tea, grow old, et cetera.
I keep my options and curtains open
because I have nothing to lose.
All the windows in this room
are going to betray me

## I Failed to Swoon

That wasn't very smart of you.
You need to start seeing things the way I do.
Here, let me blind you.

## Bruise Unit

Is a Scarlet a baby scar?
My bomb body tortures the bath.
Don't buy a memory foam mattress
unless you are sadistic
and hate yourself.

## Pain by Association

Once these shoes are broken in
I will never wear them again.

Isn't it funny
Desire

## I Am My Own Lapidary


Everything about me is stone
Stone face, stone arms
Stone amygdala, stone thigh bones
My gut is all stone. I pass stones.
When I pee stones, blood comes out
I do not own any surfaces
Nothing I bleed on is mine
I get displayed all the time
I shit pebbles like a marble rabbit
I'm unpredictable
Principal investigator and provider
of care to all stones
My dog is a stone
He's cute for a stone
I'm going to take care of him
It will be so brutal

## Dominion Piece

My dumb tail won't stop wagging for its captor
They say a body is a house
but I am not a house
My tragic face
is a terrible awning

## My Surfaces, My Services

He asked for pictures of my room
I showed him my chair
My bedposts
My curtains
My carpet
Before you ask
No
They don't match

## Come to My Cremation

Liminality sounds like a cop-out to me
Either you throw yourself into something,
or you don't. If my house caught on fire
and I could only save one thing,
I'd save the fire.

## Interview with a Vampire

Does the sight of blood repel you?
Yes, and I regret that.
Yes, and I do not regret that.
No, and I regret that.
No, and I do not regret that.

## The Rigger and the Rope Bunny

Why am I in pain
I didn't make any sudden movements
or did I

**I Love New York**

Everyone who wears that T-shirt is a liar.

## Those Who Hate the Scent of Their Children

My desire for life is, um, limited.
I'm romantic, like a virus –
one dies so that the other can live.
I have no, um, dignity.
If you threw me a chocolate,
I would eat it.
If you threw me another one,
I would eat it.
If you threw me another one,
I would eat it.
If you threw me another one,
I would eat it.
If you threw me another one,
I would eat it.
If you threw me another one,
I would vomit
and then I'd eat it,
and eat the chocolate, too.

## Aggression Quest

I found a man capable of great tenderness
and, by association, great deceit.
Yesterday morning, he broke the neck of a swan.
By evening, they'd crowned him king.

## Penance Dress

I keep you at a safe distance –
a stone's throw away from harm.
I wear a "Brunettes Have More Fun" T-shirt
but I'm a blonde.

## Dungeon Poem

Last night my loved called me diabolical

These words like handcuffs
tied to my radiator

My beautiful lover

My beautiful, manacled
lover.

## Everything Goth Is Perverse

Who can permit themselves
to glorify darkness and pain
to beautify darkness and pain
I can do nothing with darkness and pain
I have too much of it
It is unwieldy and ugly
and financially unviable
and it is also mine, which is worse
What does a thief do with that which is theirs
I mean, morally and legally theirs
My poor subjectivity
I can't give it away
I'm too selfish and secretive
Too mercenary and arrogant
Too clumsy and weak and dumb
I'm simply too full of
Darkness and pain
Glorious darkness and pain
Beautiful darkness and pain

**Misery Competition**

I'll tell you what's goth
I bleed so much
my shit has turned completely black
Black, like the heart on your T-shirt
Black, like the world in your songs

**Dear Customer**

Who will look after you when I'm gone
Who will look after you huh
Who will look after you

## Make It Stop

The dog is out in the yard
and it is maybe safe
and it is maybe not safe
and the gate is a clanging
and the night is a nuisance
and the dog is out in the yard.

## Choose Your Fighter

I have received, but not eaten,
a box of chocolates.
The insides are made almost
exclusively of cherry,
save for a little stone
they forgot at the factory.

## New York Loves You

I once bought a dog
and then the dog owned me.
Capital yields like that. Love, too.
God's dick was soft when he made you.
Flattery will get you nowhere
except my house,
my bed,
and my life.

**Failure to Connect**

Caught a glance like a cold
A sneeze
Forgive me

## Gag on the Dead and Call It Breathing

My existence is loud
The subway denizens frown upon it
I wear loud shoes to assert my presence
I walk around town with maximum anger
I empty my lungs on the dead
and then I inhale again

My existence is loud

My existence is loud

## In Each Nightmare I Survive

Multiple fleshes
Chained and whipped
Is the beach ready for my body?
Kicked in the stomach
Coffee-ground vomit
What are the conditions
for unconditional love

## Dazzling Lull

Are you ready for the greatest show on earth
Let's hang out in shit weather
There's no such thing as an honest burger
or uncomplicated dick

## Forgot the Attachment

If you leave this book feeling exfoliated,
you are wrong.

**House Music**

The clanging of gates
The creaking of stairs
The running of faucets
The shuffling of chairs

## I Sucked Down Death

and I kept him inside
He stayed for breakfast
I polished his shoes
I used my best towel
It was my mother's towel
but I guess it's his towel now

## All These Psychoses Are Driving Me Crazy

What are you
the Kennedy assassination
because I don't care whether you're staged or real
I envy Kennedy
Not the dead one
but the one in the pink dress
played by Natalie Portman.
Can you even call her a Kennedy
Oh, the things I'd do
for a blood-stained dress

## My Sisters Are My Pallbearers

Nothing tender about an "accident"
There's a cadaver in everything I write.

## None of My Powers Are Secret

I wouldn't want to be a blonde in a horror movie
I wouldn't want to be a blonde at a festival
I wouldn't want to be a blonde in the darkness
I wouldn't want to be a blonde in my house

## Genital Clown

Your tyrant's secret weapon is you

## Safe Combination

Why are you afraid of the trees
The trees never harmed anyone
They can't move, you see
And they've been here since
before you were born
If you could see their rings, you'd believe me
Don't be afraid of the trees
The trees never harmed anyone

**Puppy Season**

The night I sent you pictures of my breasts
and you ignored them, there were garbage bags
hanging in the trees.

## The Emperor's New Noose

They're setting off fire crackers
They're setting off fire crackers in my street
And in the hallway of my house
My body is lying to me
It's telling me there's a war going on
But there's no war going on at all

## Those Who Keep Their Children Small

I'd choose your first-born last
Make them feel it, kind of
The not being special at all
The being perceived as simple
Boring, even
Could it stomach that, you think
Or should I hide the medicine
⌈Cover up all sharp edges
⌊And tape the windows shut
Poor thing, do you think
✳Art is more important than dying

## Disaster Is a Verb

Bought some bread
Took a train
Swam a lap
Nearly drowned
Met a man
Got undressed
Sucked a cock
Lost a friend
Ate a meal
Took a cab
Brushed my teeth
Washed my hair
Smelled his cigarette
Didn't sleep

**Women's Prison**

I'm not afraid of consequences

Are consequences afraid of me

## Emergency Burden

A dream in which I wet myself in public,
the urine dripping on my fancy leather shoes
I'm eating a big moth with my bare teeth,
all gummy
while my ex rides by on a skateboard, asking
Whazzzzzzzup

**In the New Year I Will Be Stone Cold**


It's New Year's Day
I found an old lover's underwear in my closet
I smelled it
Didn't feel a thing
In the new year I'm going to be stone cold
In the new year I'm going to be tough as nails
Every day will be garbage day
and none of my poems will be sentimental

**An Us**


Asshole
Why did you leave
You made me indecent
And you made me cruel
I step on snails because I can
I killed a moth because I'm selfish
Asshole
I wish you lonely
I wish you Ten of Swords reversed
And the shock of a new day
Every day
Why did you leave
Where have you gone
Asshole
Asshole

## Tar and Feathers

I don't need a Red Bull
Every time a tyrant dies my amygdala gets wings

## Marnie's Sweater

Marnie's mother says to Marnie:
When I was fifteen I really wanted this sweater
It belonged to a boy I knew
He said I could have it
If he could have me
And so I let him have me
And that is how I got my sweater
And that is how I got you, too

## Haptic Sin

I had a violent lover
And now I am a violent lover
One by one we infect each other anew

## Sometimes I Forget I'm a Target

I watch Natalie Portman die on-screen

On-screen I watch Natalie Portman die

## Acknowledgments

With gratitude to Dominic Jaeckle at *Hotel*, Astra Papachristodoulou at *WhyNow*, Owen Vince at *Minor Literatures*, and Ben Fama at *Wonder* for previously publishing some of these poems.

To Peter Gizzi and Jack Underwood, for all the generous words.

And to Richard, Vikki, Maria, and Tommy at Dostoyevsky Wannabe, for giving this book a pulse.

I dedicate this book to all my friends.

## About the author

Nadia de Vries is the author of *Dark Hour* (Dostoyevsky Wannabe, 2018). She lives and works in Amsterdam, the Netherlands.

www.nadiadevries.com

Printed in Great Britain
by Amazon

40852884R00037